Momentous Materials

Glass

by Trudy Becker

FOCUS READERS.

BEACON

www.focusreaders.com

Focus Readers is distributed by North Star Editions:
sales@northstareditions.com | 888-417-0195

Produced for Focus Readers by Red Line Editorial.

Photographs ©: Shutterstock Images, cover, 1, 4, 7, 8, 11, 13, 16, 18, 21, 22, 25, 27, 29; iStockphoto, 14–15

Library of Congress Cataloging-in-Publication Data
Names: Becker, Trudy, author.
Title: Glass / by Trudy Becker.
Description: Mendota Heights, MN : Focus Readers, [2024] | Series:
   Momentous materials | Includes bibliographical references and index. |
   Audience: Grades 2-3
Identifiers: LCCN 2023033086 (print) | LCCN 2023033087 (ebook) | ISBN
   9798889980322 (hardcover) | ISBN 9798889980759 (paperback) | ISBN
   9798889981572 (ebook pdf) | ISBN 9798889981183 (hosted ebook)
Subjects: LCSH: Glass--Juvenile literature.
Classification: LCC TP857.3 .B43 2024 (print) | LCC TP857.3 (ebook) | DDC
   666/.1--dc23/eng/20230822
LC record available at https://lccn.loc.gov/2023033086
LC ebook record available at https://lccn.loc.gov/2023033087

Printed in the United States of America
Mankato, MN
012024

About the Author

Trudy Becker lives in Minneapolis, Minnesota. She likes exploring new places and loves anything involving books.

Table of Contents

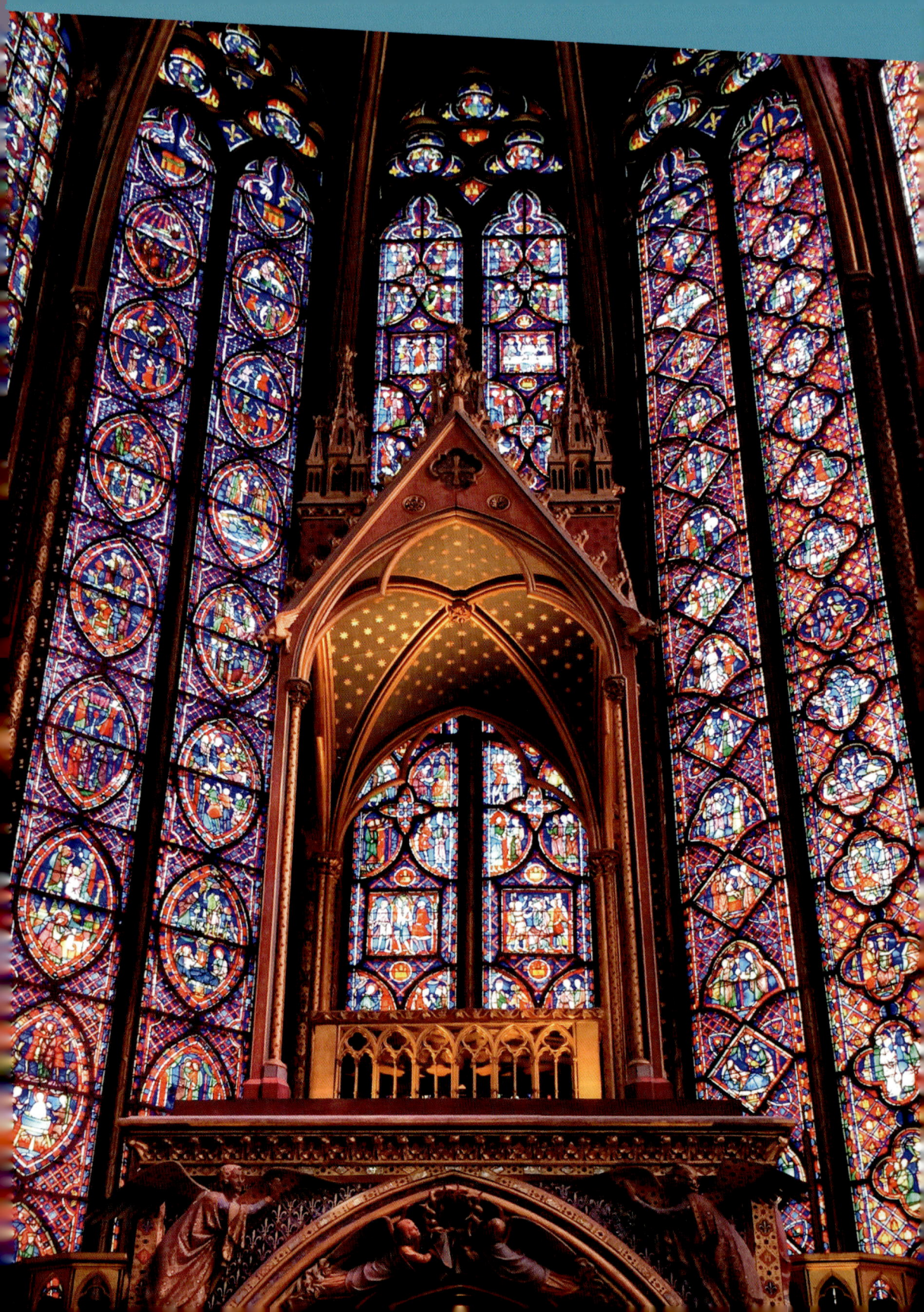

Chapter 1

A World of Glass

A girl and her mom are visiting a new city. It's a hot day. To cool off, they go inside an old church. The church has many stained-glass windows. The sunlight makes the glass glow.

 **Paris, France, has many stained-glass windows.**

The girl looks at the windows more closely. Each one is made of many small pieces of glass. The shining blocks of color create beautiful pictures.

The girl and her mom go back outside. To cool off, they buy sodas. The glass bottles feel cold in their hands.

Did You Know?

More than 600 billion glass bottles are produced every year.

Finally, it's time to go back to the hotel. So, the girl's mom checks her phone to find the way. She touches the glass screen while she looks. On this trip, and every day, glass is all around.

Chapter 2

History of Glass

Humans have been making glass for thousands of years. It was first made in the Middle East. Historians think people might have discovered glass while making other things with metal.

 **Some museums display ancient glass bottles.**

All glass uses the same three parts. Those parts are sand, ash, and **lime**. To make glass, a person heats up the three parts. Next, the person shapes the melted form. When it cools, it is glass.

Long ago, glass had a few different purposes. People used glass for beads and decorations. People made bottles and vases, too. Glassmakers used a variety of **molds**. That way, they could form glass into many different shapes.

 A glassmaker's workshop has many molds.

In some places, the methods for glassmaking were a big secret. Glass was also expensive. So, only rich people could afford it. But over the years, glassmaking methods spread. More and more people began to do it.

Workers also started making glass ingots. An ingot is a solid block of material. People sent the ingots to other places. That way, the glass could be reshaped later.

Over time, glassmakers found new methods. Some people learned how to shape glass with

Did You Know?

Some scientists test glass from **archaeological** sites. That way, they can learn more about how people lived long ago.

 Venice, Italy, is famous for its glass shops.

glassblowing. Others started making flat sheets of glass for windows. Eventually, people used glass to create eyeglasses and telescopes.

Seeing with Glass

Light bends when it shines through glass. The shape of the glass changes the light's direction. In the 1200s, scientists thought that might be useful. So, they made different types of glass. Next, they shined light through each type. Using what they learned, scientists invented eyeglasses.

Eyeglasses bend light. They direct the light toward the correct part of the eye. They make images bigger, too. That helps people see better. These same ideas helped people invent the telescope.

The telescope was invented in the early 1600s.

Chapter 3

Modern Methods

Today, the basics of glassmaking are the same as in the past. People still use sand, ash, and lime. Even so, glassmaking methods have improved. New tools have made some of these changes possible.

Glassmaking can be dangerous because it involves high temperatures.

 Glassmaking furnaces can reach temperatures of more than 2,000 degrees Fahrenheit (1,093°C).

For example, modern furnaces are stronger. They can get to higher temperatures faster. So, people can make glass more quickly.

New **technologies** can also change the look and shape of glass. For instance, glassmakers can create glass in more colors. They can also make glass more **transparent** than before. Instead of looking cloudy, modern glass is usually clear. Glass can be made into very thin pieces now, too.

Did You Know?

Glass expands when it is heated. It shrinks when it is cooled.

Glass can be flattened. It can be very smooth. These things were difficult in the past.

The strength of glass is another modern improvement. In the past, glass was easy to break. But now, people can make glass much tougher. To do so, the glass is dipped in melted salt. This makes the surface harder to shatter. That way, the glass can be used in more things. Smartphone screens are one example.

 Modern glass is strong enough to be used as walls.

In the past, most glassmaking was done by individuals and small groups. But now, most glass is made by big companies. They produce glass using machines instead of making it by hand.

Chapter 4

The Glass Age

All over the world, glass is part of daily life. Some uses have not changed for thousands of years. People still wear glass beads. They still make vases. Glass is still used for decorations, too.

 **A glassmaker shapes glass into a colorful vase.**

Other uses have changed over time. For many years, eyeglasses were expensive. Only rich people could afford them. But new glassmaking methods have made eyeglasses less expensive. Today, many people have them.

Modern eyeglasses are powerful. They are also easy to **customize**. That has made them more popular. The same is true for telescopes and microscopes. Both became important scientific tools. They

 **More than half of people in the United States wear eyeglasses.**

have helped scientists make many discoveries.

Simple forms of glass have improved over time. For example, today's windows are flatter, clearer, and stronger than ever before.

These types of windows used to be rare. But now they are everywhere.

Glass is part of many electronic devices. Phones, computers, and TVs have glass screens. Glass is also used to make **fiber-optic** cables. These cables help people get faster internet service.

Did You Know?

Most glass is easy to **recycle**. It can be melted down. Then people can shape it and use it again.

 The Shard is a glass-covered skyscraper in London, England.

Long ago, humans had the Stone Age and the Iron Age. Today, glass is all around. Perhaps the current era should be called the Glass Age!

FOCUS ON
Glass

Write your answers on a separate piece of paper.

1. Write a paragraph describing several modern uses of glass.

2. What is your favorite way to use glass in your daily life? Why?

3. What is one of the main ingredients of glass?
- **A.** sand
- **B.** windows
- **C.** furnaces

4. Why is it useful to make glass in very thin pieces?
- **A.** Thin pieces are harder to break than thick pieces.
- **B.** Thin pieces weigh less than thick pieces.
- **C.** Thin pieces come in different colors than thick pieces.

5. What does **variety** mean in this book?

*Glassmakers used a **variety** of molds. That way, they could form glass into many different shapes.*

    A. people who do a job
    B. a type of strong glass
    C. many different kinds

6. What does **furnaces** mean in this book?

*For example, modern **furnaces** are stronger. They can get to higher temperatures faster.*

    A. machines that fix things
    B. machines that heat things
    C. machines that cool things

Answer key on page 32.

Glossary

archaeological
Having to do with the study of the ancient past, often by digging up buildings or objects from long ago.

customize
To build something for a particular person.

fiber-optic
Thin strands of glass that can send information using light.

glassblowing
Shaping glass items by blowing air through a tube.

lime
A material made by heating limestone or chalk and then adding water.

molds
Empty containers that are filled with hot liquid. The liquid takes a specific shape when it cools and hardens.

recycle
To take apart an old item and make the pieces into something new.

technologies
Machines and devices created using science.

transparent
Clear or letting light through.

To Learn More

BOOKS

Jacobson, Ryan, and Glen Mullaly. *How Do Telescopes, Binoculars, and Microscopes Work?* Mankato, MN: The Child's World, 2022.

Peterson, Christy. *Cutting-Edge Hubble Telescope Data*. Minneapolis: Lerner Publications, 2020.

Ward, Lesley. *The Science of Glass*. Huntington Beach, CA: Teacher Created Materials, 2019.

NOTE TO EDUCATORS

Visit **www.focusreaders.com** to find lesson plans, activities, links, and other resources related to this title.

Index

Answer Key: 1. Answers will vary; **2.** Answers will vary; **3.** A; **4.** B; **5.** C; **6.** B